GOODBYE, JEEPERS

What to expect when your pet dies

by Nancy Loewen

illustrated by Christopher Lyles

One Saturday morning, I poured my cereal. I poured my milk. Then I stopped.

Something was missing.

Usually, the rustling of the cereal bag made Jeepers squeak. Jeepers was my guinea pig. He squeaked whenever he heard the crinkling sound of plastic bags. He thought he was getting a treat.

I rustled the cereal bag again. Nothing.

I went to Jeepers's cage and lifted up his hutch. He was curled into a ball. His eyes were open … but he wasn't looking at me.

"Mum! Dad!" I shouted. "Something's wrong with Jeepers!"

3

I ran into my room. After a few minutes
Dad came in. "I'm sorry," he said,
"but Jeepers is—"

"Dead," I said. "I know.
I'm not a baby."

My lips felt funny all of a sudden.

"It's OK to cry," Dad said, putting his arm around
me. "It might make you feel better."

But I pressed my lips together. I didn't want to cry.

At first, you might pretend that your pet hasn't died, or that you don't care. That's OK. But so is crying. There is no right or wrong way to act when a pet dies. Grief is different for everyone.

5

I was so happy when the doorbell rang. I didn't want to think about death and all that sad stuff. Anton and his cousin asked me to go to the playground with them. So I did.

We went down the spiral slide 10 times.

We hung upside down from the monkey bars and played naughts and crosses in the sand.

I hardly thought about Jeepers at all.

Grief isn't a single feeling. It can be many feelings that come and go over time. And it's OK to think of things other than your pet. It's even OK to have fun! It doesn't mean that you didn't love your pet.

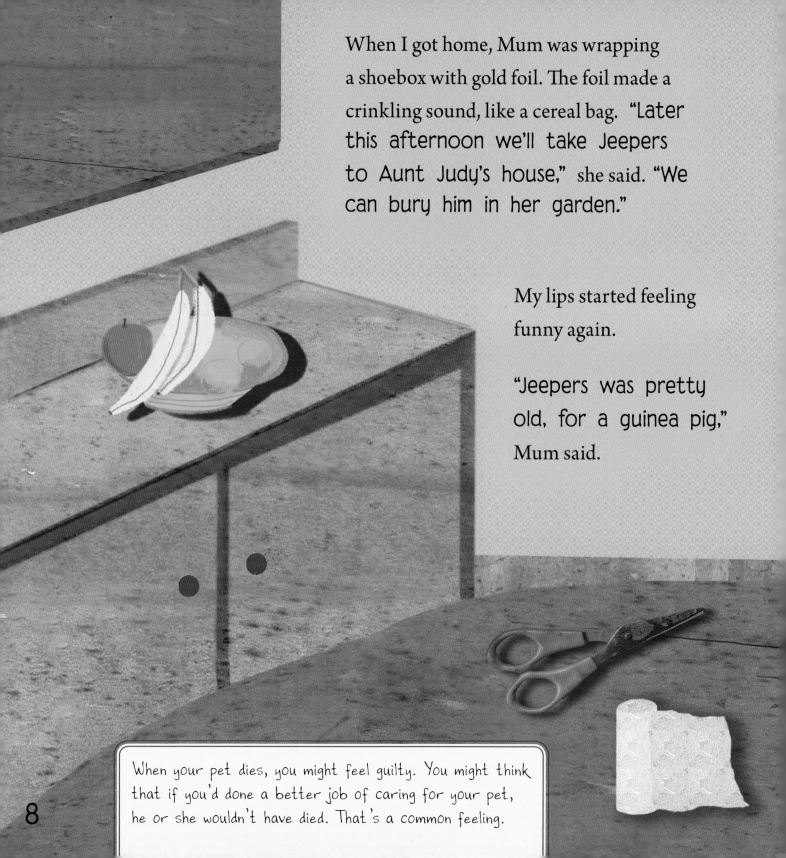

When I got home, Mum was wrapping a shoebox with gold foil. The foil made a crinkling sound, like a cereal bag. "Later this afternoon we'll take Jeepers to Aunt Judy's house," she said. "We can bury him in her garden."

My lips started feeling funny again.

"Jeepers was pretty old, for a guinea pig," Mum said.

When your pet dies, you might feel guilty. You might think that if you'd done a better job of caring for your pet, he or she wouldn't have died. That's a common feeling.

8

"So it wasn't my fault?" I asked. I thought about the times I'd forgotten to give Jeepers fresh water.

Mum hugged me. "No, Jeepers had a good life here, with all of us. I'll miss him."

"I'll miss him too!" I burst out, and we both started to cry.

9

When Mum and I had finished crying,
we made Jeepers the coolest box ever.

We lined the box with a comfy towel.
Mum took Jeepers out of his cage and
carefully placed him inside. At first I
didn't want to touch him. But then I did.
His body was cool and stiff, but his fur
still felt as soft as ever.

On the bus to Aunt Judy's house, a lady across the aisle smiled at me. "That's a beautiful box," she said. "You must be carrying something very special in there."

I didn't feel like smiling back.

"Our pet guinea pig died," Mum explained. "We're taking him to my sister's garden to bury him."

"I'm very sorry for your loss," the lady said to me in a kind voice.

Suddenly everyone was looking at my gold box.

"What was his name?" a girl asked.

"Jeepers," I replied.

"Could he do any tricks?" a boy asked.

Talking about your pet is a way of honouring him or her. You'll feel better, remembering the good times and knowing that your pet won't be forgotten.

"Not really," I said. "But he could squeak louder than anything."

"Once he squeaked so loudly I thought the smoke alarm was going off!" Dad said.

Everyone around us laughed. I smiled a little.

"I used to have a guinea pig called Patches," the boy said. "I had to be careful or she'd nibble my hair."

"I had a dog called Patches!" the girl said.

Death is a part of living. We can't avoid it. Everyone has, or will have, experiences with death. It's one of the things that draws us closer together.

A man with a hat put down his newspaper. "My cat, Pickles, used to sleep on my head," he said.

By the time we had reached our stop, it seemed like the whole bus knew about Jeepers. And we'd heard stories of all sorts of amazing pets.

When I got off the bus, I still felt sad. But not as sad as before.

I waved goodbye as the bus rolled away.

And then we buried Jeepers.

Pets that have died might be buried in gardens or pet cemeteries. They might be cremated, and their ashes scattered in a special place. Treating your pet's body with care and respect can be an important part of saying goodbye.

19

That night our flat felt so empty.
It felt like that for a long time.

Sometimes I forgot that Jeepers had gone. In the morning, I'd rustle the cereal bag and listen for his squeak.

After school, I'd save him the last bite of my apple.

My teacher, Mr Dennis, and I talked about Jeepers a lot. Mr Dennis is a good listener. He used to have a pet tarantula when he was little. He knows what it feels like when a pet dies.

Mum and Dad told me that when I was ready, I could have another pet. "HOW will I know when I'm ready?" I asked.

"You'll know," Mum said. "It's when you think about Jeepers and feel happy that you knew him, instead of sad that you lost him."

I hope that time comes soon. This place is so quiet without him.

Glossary

cemetery place where people or animals are buried; a graveyard

cremate expose a body to high heat, which turns it into ash

grief process we go through when we experience death or another kind of loss; when we grieve, we might feel sadness, anger, loneliness and other emotions

guilty feeling of having done something wrong; feeling shame

honour show respect for someone or something

Website

pbskids.org/itsmylife/emotions/death/article11.html

The death of a pet is very different from the death of a person, but we can still learn a lot about grieving from these experiences.

Read more

Goodbye Mog, Judith Kerr (Harper Collins Children's Books, 2003)

I Miss My Pet, Pat Thomas (Wayland, 2013)

Sad (Dealing with Feeling…), Isabel Thomas (Raintree, 2014)

Index

Look for all the books in the Life's Challenges series:

Goodbye, Jeepers

The Night Dad Went to Prison

Saying Goodbye to Uncle Joe

Weekends with Dad

Raintree is an imprint of Capstone Global Library Limited, a company incorporated in England and Wales having its registered office at 264 Banbury Road, Oxford, OX2 7DY – Registered company number: 6695582

www.raintree.co.uk
myorders@raintree.co.uk

Text © Capstone Global Library Limited 2016
The moral rights of the proprietor have been asserted.

Editor: Jill Kalz
Designer: Alison Thiele
Art Director: Nathan Gassman
Production Specialist: Sarah Bennett
The illustrations in this book were created with collage and enhanced digitally.

ISBN 978 1 4747 2471 5
20 19 18 17 16
10 9 8 7 6 5 4 3 2 1

British Library Cataloguing in Publication Data
A full catalogue record for this book is available from the British Library.

Acknowledgements
Thanks to our advisers for their expertise, research and advice:

Michele Goyette-Ewing, PhD Director of Psychology Training Yale Child Study Center

Terry Flaherty, PhD Professor of English Minnesota State University, Mankato

Every effort has been made to contact copyright holders of material reproduced in this book. Any omissions will be rectified in subsequent printings if notice is given to the publisher.

All the internet addresses (URLs) given in this book were valid at the time of going to press. However, due to the dynamic nature of the internet, some addresses may have changed, or sites may have changed or ceased to exist since publication. While the author and publisher regret any inconvenience this may cause readers, no responsibility for any such changes can be accepted by either the author or the publisher.

Made in China